The First Day of School for Theodore Rex

By Gina Shaw
Illustrated by Jed Henry

Scholastic Inc.

Theodore Rex woke up early in the morning. He washed his face and brushed all sixty of his razor-sharp teeth.

"Son, are you ready for your first day of school?" his dad asked.

"I CAN'T WAIT!" Theodore Rex roared at the top of his lungs.

Theodore Rex always roared when he was excited.
"Not so loud, son," his dad said. "I can hear you."

Theodore Rex planned to go by his nickname, T. rex, at school. He had been waiting all summer for the first day of school.

He stretched his long legs as he walked with his dad. He couldn't wait to make new friends and play tag at recess. He was the fastest dinosaur on his block.

When T. rex and his dad arrived at school, the classroom was filled with all kinds of dinosaurs. He felt scared and excited at the same time.

He said good-bye to his dad and took his seat. He listened quietly to his new teacher, Mrs. Hadrosaur.

The bell for recess finally rang! T. rex and all the other dinosaurs raced outside. Everyone yelled and made noise.

But when T. rex let out an excited ROAR,
the other dinosaurs turned and ran away!

T. rex stomped over to Maya Maiasaura. She had a duck-billed face like their teacher, Mrs. Hadrosaur. She was eating plants with her sister Molly.

Blech! T. rex thought. He did not like eating plants! Still, he wanted to make a friend.

"HI!" T. rex roared.
"DO YOU WANT TO PLAY WITH ME?"

Maya and Molly shrieked and ran away.
T. rex felt sad.

T. rex heard a rustling in a nearby bush. He walked over to take a look. He saw Billy Bambiraptor. Billy was small and looked like a bird.

"HI!" T. rex roared.

"DO YOU WANT TO PLAY WITH ME?"

Billy was so frightened that he ran off without saying a word. He lost a few feathers during his escape. One landed on T. rex's nose.

AHHH-CHOOOOOO!

T. rex felt sad.

T. rex spotted Andy Ankylosaurus in the school yard munching plants. He was short and wide. He was covered in bony plates that looked like armor. Andy did not seem to notice T. rex.

"HI!" T. rex roared.

"DO YOU WANT TO PLAY WITH ME?"

Andy quickly raised his tail club. He swung at T. rex and just missed his head! T. rex was shocked and hurt.

"Why did you do that?" T. rex asked. "I'm just trying to make friends."

Andy looked surprised. “T. rex,” he said, “you scare all of us with your loud roar. If you want to make friends, you need to lower your voice.”

That day, school became much easier for T. rex.
He stopped roaring at everyone.

He and Andy became friends.
They played tag with Maya and Molly.

At the end of the day, T. rex's dad came to pick him up. He asked T. rex how his first day of school was.

In his new and quieter tone of voice, T. rex said, "It was great. I can't wait to come back tomorrow and see all of my friends again! I like my duck-billed teacher, Mrs. Hadrosaur, too."

Mrs. Hadrosaur overheard T. rex.
She smiled and let out a loud "Quack!"

Father and son ROARED with laughter
all the way home.

A VISUAL GLOSSARY

Ankylosaur

Hadrosaur

Armor

Maiasaura

Bambiraptor

T. rex

Tail club

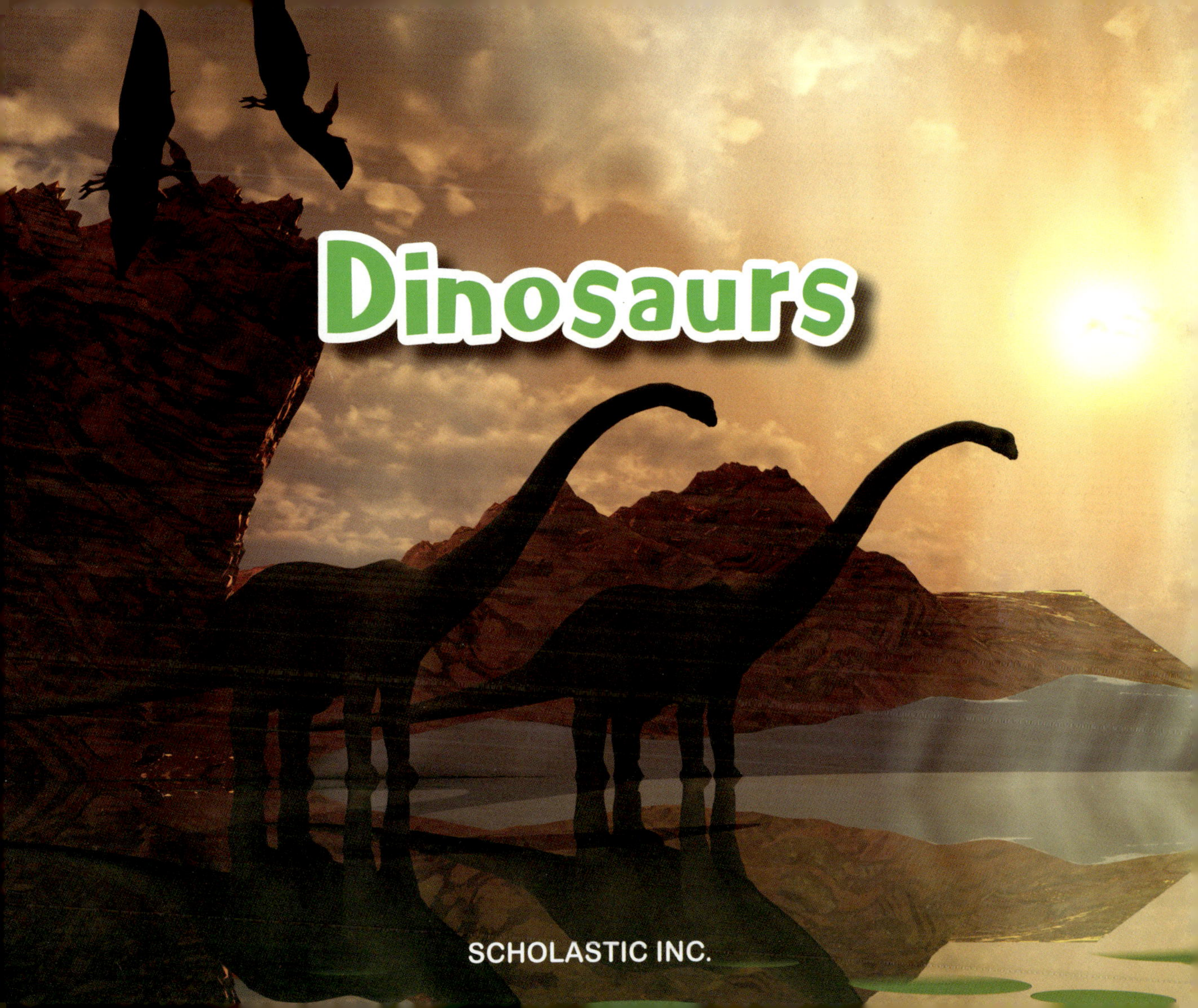

Dinosaurs

SCHOLASTIC INC.

Contents

Meet T. rex

Roarrrrrrrr!

This is Tyrannosaurus rex.
(tye-RAN-uh-SAWR-us REKS).
Some people call
Tyrannosaurus rex
"T. rex."

T. rex was big. Big. Big. T. rex was strong, too. This dinosaur ate any animal in its path. Watch out for T. rex!

A man named Barnum Brown discovered T. rex.

huge head
long tail
to keep its
balance
sixty sharp
teeth
short arms and
hands with two
fingers
long, strong legs
toes with sharp claws

T. rex had:

- a huge head.
- sixty sharp teeth that could crush bone.
- long, strong legs that could run up to 25 miles per hour.
- toes with sharp claws.
- a long tail to keep its balance.
- short arms and hands with two fingers.

T. rex was a deadly hunter.

A T.rex could eat 500 pounds in one bite!

Dinosaur Times

T. rex lived long, long ago. The world was very different back then.

Most flying reptiles were a kind of pterosaur.

Dinosaurs ruled the land. Other big reptiles ruled the air and the sea.

Dinosaurs went extinct about 65 million years ago.

Dinosaurs died out before people lived on Earth.
How do we know about them?

Herd of Argentinosaurus

Fossils Tell Tales

Fossils tell us about dinosaurs.

What are fossils? Fossils are bones, shells, footprints, and other traces of plants and animals that are saved, or preserved, in rock. Scientists have even found fossils of dinosaur poop!

Fossils of dinosaur poop are called coprolites.

Fossilized dinosaur skeleton

Most fossils are found in rocks.

Fossils tell us stories of the past. They tell us where dinosaurs lived. They tell us how dinosaurs moved. They tell us what dinosaurs ate. Studying fossils can tell us many things about what the world was like before humans lived.

Living with T. rex

More than 1,300 kinds of dinosaurs lived on Earth. But only some lived in the same period as T. rex. Maiasaura (MY-yuh-SAWR-uh) means "good mother lizard." These dinosaurs ate plants. They lived in groups and took care of their young.

Hadrosaurs like Maiasaura are called duck-billed dinosaurs.

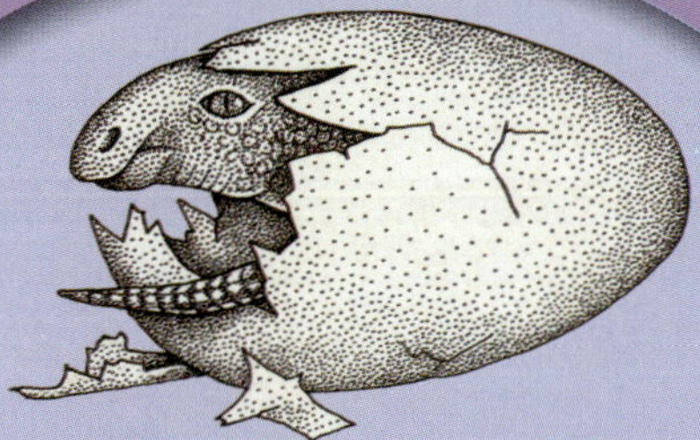

Maiasaura hatching from an egg

Maiasaura and her young

Bambiraptor (BAM-bee-RAP-tor) weighed just seven pounds. But it was quick. This little hunter probably ate lizards and insects.

Scientists think Bambiraptors were covered in feathers!

Bambiraptor feinbergi

Ankylosaurs (ang-KILE-uh-sawrs) ate plants. But they were built for battle. Their tough, bony plates acted like armor and kept them safe. One whack with their tail club could send a T. rex flying through the air.

Ankylosaurs were very big but had tiny brains.

Ankylosaurus

Dinosaurs Today?

T. rex is long gone. But birds are everywhere. Scientists think birds evolved from dinosaurs. Does this bird look like a dinosaur to you?

Ostrich feet

African ostrich and her chicks

Glossary

- **dinosaur:** a kind of reptile that lived on land a long time ago.
- **evolve:** to slowly change over time.
- **fossil:** bones, shells, footprints, and other traces of plants and animals that are saved, or preserved, in rock.
- **reptile:** an animal that has scaly skin, a backbone, and lungs.

This Book
Belongs To:

T. rex

Dinosaurs Ruled the Earth

Find a sticker that matches the shape in each sentence.
Put the sticker on the blank line. Then read the sentence.

1. Dinosaurs were not lizards, but the word *dinosaur* means "terrible ____________."

2. Maiasaura means "good mother lizard." These dinosaurs ate ____________.

3. We have found dinosaur bones, teeth, and footprints called ____________.

4. Scientists think that some birds like the ____________ evolved from dinosaurs.

5. More than 1,300 kinds of dinosaurs once roamed the ____________.

6. Ankylosaurus could have used its tail club to knock down a ____________.

7. Bambiraptor was a tiny dinosaur that ate ____________.

T. rex skeleton

What Does Theodore Rex Do Before School?

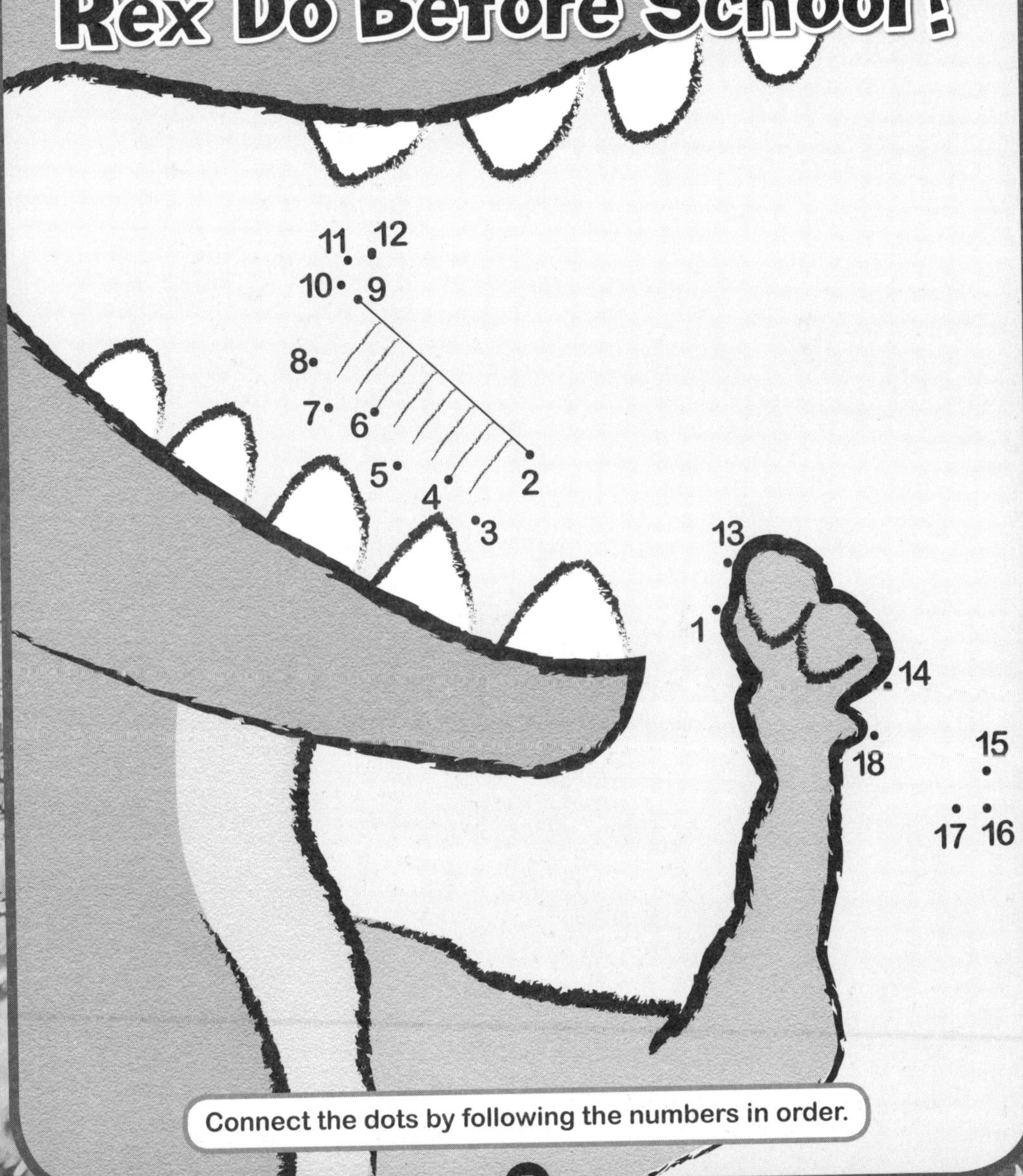

Connect the dots by following the numbers in order.

Gigantosaurus

Word Search

Find these words and circle them.
HINT: The words go across or down.

arms	bone	fierce	fossils	gentle	legs
meat	plants	rocks	skeleton	teeth	tools

K	E	F	K	N	A	F	E	G	C
P	A	R	M	S	I	I	P	E	M
R	G	Q	S	W	G	E	F	N	I
O	J	M	K	B	F	R	O	T	P
C	N	E	E	T	W	C	S	L	L
K	T	A	L	O	U	E	S	E	A
S	E	T	E	O	Q	B	I	Z	N
R	E	C	T	L	S	O	L	K	T
L	T	M	O	S	Z	N	S	E	S
T	H	H	N	S	L	E	G	S	V

Spinosaurus

Picture Matching Fun

Find the matching stickers. Then, using the letters on the stickers, spell out the words on the lines below.

1.

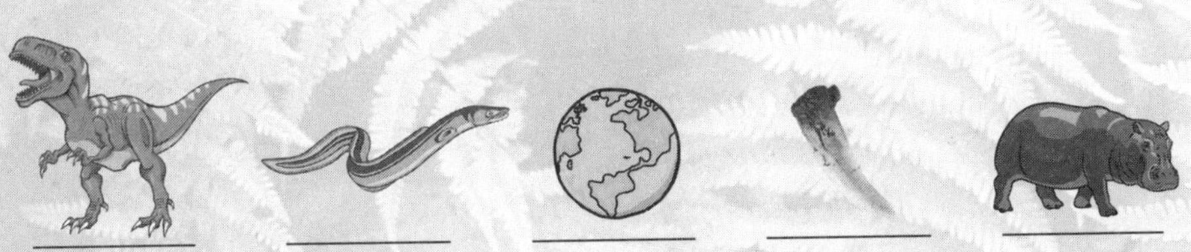

2.

3.

4.

Deinonychus

Make a Match!

Can you match the picture with the correct word?
Draw a line from the picture on the left to the word on the right.

Tyrannosaurus rex

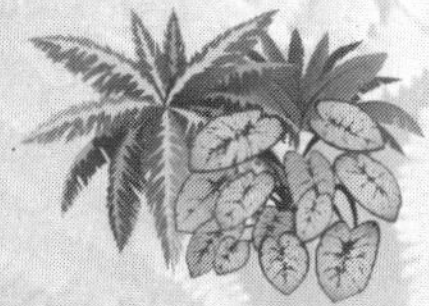

Fossil

Ankylosaurus

Plants

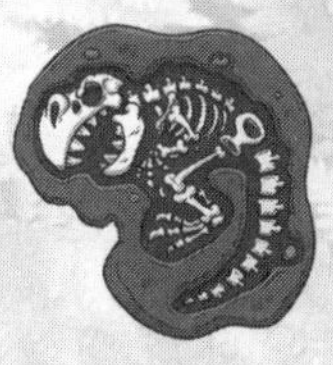

Bird

Insects

Diabloceratops

Which dinosaur is munching on plants?

Connect the dots by following the numbers in order.

Camarasaurus

Word Search

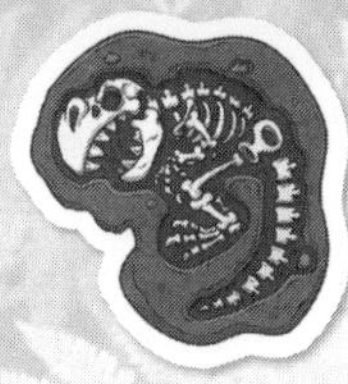

Find these words and circle them.
HINT: The words go across or down.

Earth	eggs	extinct	feathers	frill	gigantic
jaws	prey	scales	shapes	sizes	small

E G G S S G S S K L
E W S F C P H F G I
X G F E A W A O S J
T I R A L Z P Q M A
I G I T E X E E A W
N A L H S Y S A L S
C N L E I B A R L G
T T V R Z M U T O T
L I B S E J T H Y L
V C P R S C P R E Y

Answer Key

page 3

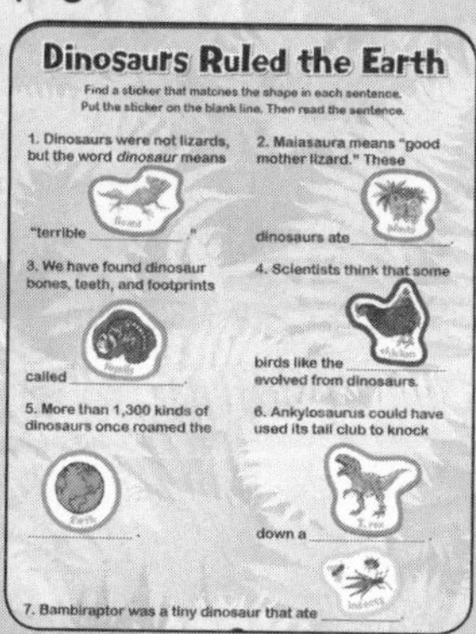

page 5

page 7

K	E	F	K	N	A	F	E	G	C
P	A	R	M	S	I	I	P	E	M
R	G	Q	S	W	G	E	F	N	I
O	J	M	K	B	F	R	O	T	P
C	N	E	E	T	W	C	S	L	L
K	T	A	L	O	U	E	S	E	A
S	E	T	E	O	Q	B	I	Z	N
R	E	C	T	L	S	O	L	K	T
L	T	M	O	S	Z	N	S	E	S
T	H	H	N	S	L	E	G	S	V

page 9

page 11

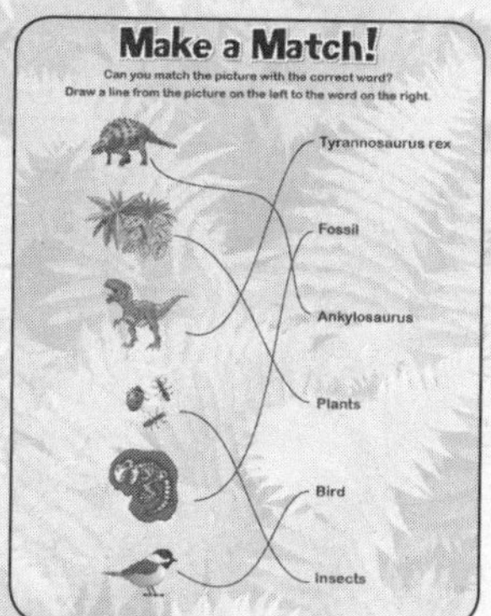

page 13

page 15

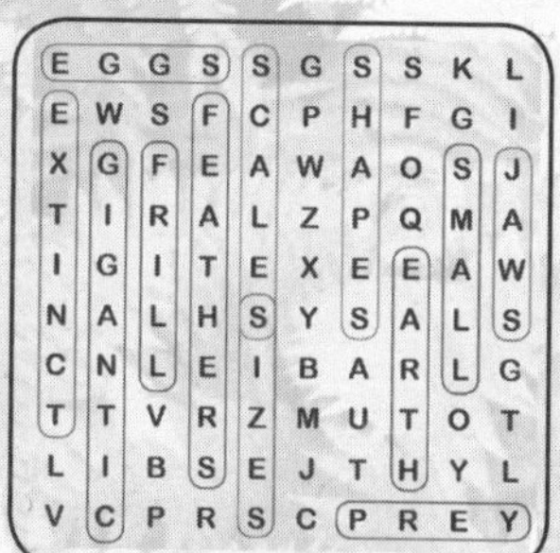

E	G	G	S	S	G	S	S	K	L
E	W	S	F	C	P	H	F	G	I
X	G	F	E	A	W	A	O	S	J
T	I	R	A	L	Z	P	Q	M	A
I	G	I	T	E	X	E	E	A	W
N	A	L	H	S	Y	S	A	L	S
C	N	L	E	I	B	A	R	L	G
T	T	V	R	Z	M	U	T	O	T
L	I	B	S	E	J	T	H	Y	L
V	C	P	R	S	C	P	R	E	Y